The  IJ Book

by Lynn Maslen Kertell
pictures by Sue Hendra and John R. Maslen

Scholastic Inc.
New York • Toronto • London • Auckland • Sydney • Mexico City • New Delhi • Hong Kong • Buenos Aires

Inchworm

ink

Inchworm's invitation to

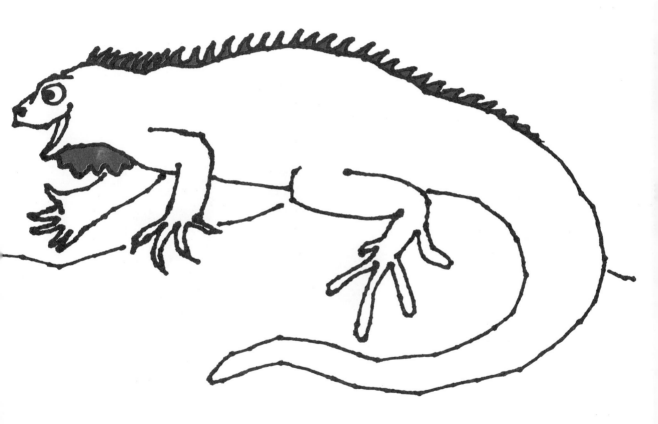

iguana is in purple ink.

Jam

jaguar

A jumping jaguar

drops his jelly beans.

Jam and jelly bean sandwiches

for jaguar, iguana, and inchworm!

Look for these **i** and **j** words in this book.

iguana	jaguar
inchworm	jam
ink	jelly bean(s)
invitation	jumping

Look for these additional **i** and **j** words in the pictures: ice cream, ice cream cone, inkwell, jacket, jars, jaws, jump rope, and jungle.